LIT1

SUSHI

THE LITTLE BOOK OF SUSHI

Text by Anna Lou Walker

An Hachette UK Company
www.hachette.co.uk

Summersdale Publishers Ltd
Part of Octopus Publishing Group Limited
Carmelite House
50 Victoria Embankment
LONDON
EC4Y 0DZ
UK

www.summersdale.com

Printed and bound in the UK

ISBN: 978-1-80007-840-6

Substantial discounts on bulk quantities of Summersdale books are available to corporations, professional associations and other organizations. For details contact general enquiries: telephone: +44 (0) 1243 771107 or email: enquiries@summersdale.com.

The
LITTLE BOOK OF
SUSHI

Rufus Cavendish

summersdale

Contents

MAKING SUSHI IS AN ART, AND EXPERIENCE IS EVERYTHING.

Nobu Matsuhisa

Introduction

If you've picked up this book, it's probable that your eyes already light up at the sight of a fresh platter of colourful sushi rolls. If so, you're in for a treat. This little book crams in fun facts, history, advice and recipes tighter than your favourite maki roll.

You might be surprised to learn that sushi's story started in China, not Japan, where it is thought to have been enjoyed since the third century BC. It's changed a lot since those early days, evolving from a way to preserve fish to a dynamic fusion cuisine with exciting variations and specialities to discover across the world. This explosion of flavours means there's now something to enjoy for everyone, from classic fresh fish nigiri to experimental sushi burritos.

Whether you want to swot up on sushi's epic history, learn some fun facts to share the next time you're sitting at your favourite sushi conveyor belt, or even become an expert sushi-maker, this book will be your guide, taking you from a sushi amateur to an *itamae* (sushi master).

THE
WONDERFUL
WORLD
OF SUSHI

Sushi's rich history spans many centuries and chapters, from humble origins as a simple food-preserving hack, to the diverse, colourful cuisine we know today. In this chapter, you'll take a journey through sushi's past, present and future, discovering what it is, where it came from and what makes it so beloved around the world.

You'll travel back to third-century BC China, to wade through the rice paddies where sushi was first dreamed up. Then you'll take a trip across the globe to learn how the cuisine conquered countries in all corners of the world. Along the way you'll learn about some jaw-dropping world records, the role an earthquake played in sushi's popularity and why Molly Ringwald played a key role in sushi's bid for world domination.

What is sushi?

Perhaps you've drooled over scenes filmed at Nori Sushi, the sushi joint favoured in *The Sopranos*. Maybe many a happy childhood weekend was spent in front of a conveyor belt of bright nigiri. Perhaps you laughed when Kim Cattrall covered her naked body in sushi in the *Sex and the City* movie. Or maybe you recall the iconic episode of *The Simpsons* where Homer enjoys sushi for the first time, only to realize that he's eaten poisonous fish and has just 24 hours left to live. However you first came to discover the joys of sushi, there's one thing for certain – it's absolutely delicious. But what exactly is it?

The word sushi refers to a Japanese dish of vinegared rice accompanied by other ingredients. This usually means raw fish, but can also refer to vegetables, seafood or even chicken – your imagination is the limit! From zesty chirashi salad bowls to sushi burritos and chunky portions of gunkan, there are now myriad forms of sushi, with thousands of potential toppings or fillings and countless presentation options, but whatever the dish, it will always rely on a base of delicious, vinegared sushi rice.

YOU HAD
ME AT NIGIRI

Who created sushi?

The origin of sushi is a rich, century-spanning story, bound in legends and ancient folklore. According to lore from ancient Japan, sushi emerged from humble origins, when an elderly woman, fearing thieves, began hiding her prized pots of rice in the nests of sea hawks. As she began to collect her pots, she found the rice had fermented and that scraps of fish from the sea hawks' hunts had mixed into the rice. To her delight, the fermented rice had also preserved the fish, and created a new, delicious cuisine that could prolong the life of seafood.

Beyond folklore, the real origins of sushi can be found in the old rice fields of China, where a dish of fermented rice and salt fish known as *narezushi* was invented in order to preserve seafood, long before the age of the fridge-freezer.

One of the earliest records of sushi appears in the Yoro Code – a set of governing rules compiled in Japan's early Nara period – in the year 718 AD. By the ninth century, sushi was rapidly gaining popularity across Japan, in part because it coincided with the rise of Buddhism, which encouraged abstaining from meat.

Restaurants famous for their sushi creations began to emerge in the 1700s, and by the end of the century there were thousands of them across Japan. It would take one very special chef named Hanaya Yohei, however, to transform the dish into the cuisine we know today...

How did sushi develop?

Born in 1799, Hanaya Yohei is the chef credited with creating the modern sushi we know and love. Hanaya was a problem solver. During the Edo Period, much of the fish used for sushi across Japan was captured from Tokyo Bay, a bay connected to the Pacific Ocean located in the southern Kantō region, which meant it was delicious when fresh but could quickly spoil. To get around this, Hanaya began marinading the catch of the day in soy sauce or vinegar before assembling his sushi, in order to extend its shelf life.

Hanaya was also keen to reduce sushi's long preparation times. He developed what was known as the *nigiri-zushi* method, which involved placing raw fish directly on top of rice balls, and hand squeezing the sushi into shape. This hand-pressed method revolutionized the way sushi was being created, taking a product that previously required several months of fermentation and transforming it into fast food.

CATCH OF THE DAY

Incredibly, 80% of tuna caught around the world is consumed in Japan. The Pacific bluefin tuna is considered auspicious during the Japanese New Year, when prices for sushi dishes containing the fish skyrocket. Sadly, the bluefin tuna is now at risk of extinction and regulations to protect the species are sorely needed across the world.

Why is sushi so popular?

Look around the next time you're eating at your favourite sushi joint and you're sure to notice a very modern trend. As each table is served, a moment of silence descends, phones are raised, and countless snaps of each aesthetically pleasing bite are uploaded to social media. According to a 2016 study, sushi is the second most Instagrammed food in the world (after pizza) and at the time of writing some 34.2 million posts have used the hashtag #Sushi on the platform.

Why is this? Perhaps it's the artistry, the craft that goes into each roll. Perhaps it's the rich history, the story held between each nori sheet. Or perhaps it's simply that it tastes so jaw-droppingly good! Whatever the reason, sushi lovers aren't short of opportunities to enjoy their favourite treats. With nearly 18,700 sushi restaurants in the US, 2,750 in the UK and a spectacular 30,000 in Japan, the world's love affair with fish and rice isn't going anywhere anytime soon.

THE *SUSHI* CLUB

The cult 1985 John Hughes classic, *The Breakfast Club*, features an important movie moment for sushi. When the film's "rich girl" Claire (Molly Ringwald) pulls out a beautiful sushi lunch set, the other kids in detention are baffled. Not only was this a sign of sushi's then reputation as a sophisticated food for the elite, but also of the beginning of its entry into mainstream US cuisine and culture.

The evolution of sushi in Japan

Sushi has come a long way from its hand-pressed and preserved origins. Pickling was crucial for people in China and Japan in those early centuries, particularly during the flooding season, when fish would become trapped in rice fields, leading to a delicious but over-bountiful haul. The excess fish (usually carp) would be rubbed with salt and pickled in a barrel over several months, before being stuffed with rice and weighed down under a heavy stone for another year.

By the eighteenth century, sushi-hungry pundits were no longer waiting a full year to crack into their supply, and the fermentation timeline shortened to just a few days. Where lactic acid, built up over the year of pickling, had previously added a sourness to the rice, people began adding vinegar to shortcut the process.

Until very recent times, sushi was enjoyed in large portions. Street vendors in nineteenth-century Tokyo would serve fish caught in the Edo Bay atop gigantic balls of rice. There was no set way to enjoy your sushi besides at speed, as the lack of refrigeration techniques meant it could go bad fast.

The invention of the refrigerator and the global economy shifted sushi forever. Now portioned far smaller than its giant ancestors, sushi is fresher and more adaptable than ever, with regional incarnations of its iconic rolls being enjoyed across the world.

The rise in sushi popularity

When asked what the biggest food breakthrough had been during his lifetime, American chef Anthony Bourdain replied, "When Americans started eating sushi and decided sometime in the seventies that raw fish was desirable, that was a big, big win."

Though it has been popular across Asia for centuries, it took a little longer for the rest of the world to catch on to sushi's appeal. During the 1970s, however, Japanese technology was taking off across the world and was synonymous with exciting innovation – a new reputation that also sparked global interest in Japanese cuisine. Once sushi became popular in the States, thanks to fusion dishes such as the California Roll, its popularity began to spread to Europe too. And the appeal has endured. UK café chain Pret A Manger claims that they sell some 30,000 packs of sushi every week, and today it's available almost anywhere: in restaurants, grocery stores, food trucks, even at petrol stations. Sushi's world domination is here to stay.

RECORD-BREAKING ROLLS

The world record for the most sushi rolls eaten in a single minute is held by American Michael Takla, who ate a whopping 471.5 grams of the stuff in August 2021. Far from your traditional fare, Takla achieved this feat noshing Alaska Rolls, which consist of fresh salmon and avocado in an uramaki style.

Sushi and sustainability

Every sushi fan knows that the most delicious dishes require super fresh fish. But the fishing industry is one of the most heavily criticized when it comes to issues of sustainability. So, what does this mean for the carbon footprint of your favourite maki roll?

According to the World Wildlife Fund, overfishing of bluefin tuna – one of the most popular sushi ingredients – has pushed the population to the brink. Scientists note that fishing levels are three times greater than what is sustainable, and the current population has been reduced to only 2.6% of its historic size. To be sure you're consuming sustainable tuna, look out for the blue MSC label when purchasing your fish.

Seaweed, meanwhile, crucial for the creation of sushi, is under threat from warming ocean temperatures. There are projects in place to counter the impact of global warming on seaweed however, including Oceans X Lab, which supports innovations in seaweed farming.

You may be surprised to learn that rice is one of the least sustainable elements in your sushi dinner. While rice paddies can provide good habitats for wildlife, they have a heavy impact on freshwater resources. However, eco-friendly rice farming techniques are on the rise to try to counter the toll of the rice industry – which is depended upon by half the world's population for food and/or income.

And finally, looking to top your nigiri roll with some tasty soy sauce? Soy is the second-biggest agricultural cause of deforestation. Sustainable soy-free fish and oyster sauces are available from brands such as Sozÿe, so shop around if you want to make your plate more eco-friendly!

LET THE GOOD
TIMES *ROLL...*

A QUAKING REVOLUTION

We have an earthquake to thank for sushi restaurants. The devastation caused in the wake of the 1923 Great Kanto earthquake caused real estate prices in Tokyo to hit an all-time low. As a result, many of the sushi chefs who had previously operated as street vendors were able to invest in property, and sushi restaurants began popping up all over the city.

Is sushi a healthy dish or indulgent treat?

Done well, sushi is a healthy food choice. It contains a rich source of protein and omega-3 fatty acids from fish, and plentiful vitamins and minerals. As with any food, however, this all depends on what exactly you're consuming, and how much. Freshly made sushi packed full of vegetables and fish is clearly going to be a lot healthier than the cream-cheese stuffed rolls you might find at an all-you-can-eat sushi buffet.

Nutritionist Nicola Shubrook suggests you "Keep rice to a minimum and look for fresh fish and sashimi-style dishes, or those wrapped in seaweed. Go easy on the soy sauce and avoid any deep-fried or mayonnaise-heavy dishes."

As sushi involves raw fish, certain kinds of bacteria, including salmonella, are a risk when eating this kind of food. The best way to avoid making yourself sick is to only consume sushi that you're confident has been prepared in a knowledgeable and sanitary environment.

Some more unusual kinds of sushi come with health risks all of their own. Fugu – Japanese pufferfish – for example, contains one of the world's most powerful toxins: tetrodotoxin. Fugu chefs require a special licence in order to prepare the dish. Despite the risks it carries, over 10,000 tons of the stuff is eaten in Japan every year!

Sushi around the world

As sushi has gained popularity around the world, the variety of its incredible fusion forms has increased exponentially. Here are some delicious fusion sushi dishes from around the world:

- **Italy** – The sushi rolls in popular restaurant Hari, in Rome, are made with courgette, lobster, pineapple, prawns and rocket. They even top some rolls with crunchy noodles in place of the more traditional fish eggs.

- **Thailand** – Thai sushi contains some ingredients that may shock sushi traditionalists. Think wagyu beef, French goose liver, pork cutlets, quail eggs and white truffle oil. Thailand is also home to deep-fried sushi rolls, available from KFC!

- **Canada** – Sushi purists, look away now. Sushi pizza has become a signature dish in Toronto. Chewy rice patties are topped with layers of sliced avocado, sliced salmon, tuna meat, mayonnaise and wasabi powder.

- **Germany** – Rollmops are Germany's answer to sushi: pickled herring fillets, rolled around a savoury filling (usually olives or gherkins) and held together with small wooden skewers.

- **USA** – San Francisco proudly claims to be the exclusive home of the "sushi burrito". Essentially a giant sushi roll, diners can choose from a range of classic sushi flavours such as yellowfin tuna and shrimp tempura.

- **Russia** – Sushi is extremely popular in Russia and is tailored to the country's tastes. Cream cheese, mayonnaise and chicken are used liberally, and sushi rolls are often topped with melted mozzarella cheese.

ALL HANDS ON DECK

All fingers and thumbs with your chopsticks?
Not to worry. Perfectly poised chopsticks
are not the only traditional way to eat sushi.
In Japan, it's both common and polite to
tuck in using your hands! Just make sure you
give them a wash before you get stuck in.

KEEP CALM
AND EAT SUSHI

The future of sushi...

Few cuisines have been through quite so many rebrands as sushi. From humble beginnings designed to preserve fish to some of the most exclusive and expensive restaurants in the world, sushi has had more iterations than Madonna has had reinventions.

Today, the biggest and most dynamic innovations in sushi all look towards the issue of sustainability. Dubbing themselves the "future of seafood", Chicago-based Aqua Cultured Foods is creating a product that looks exactly like sushi-grade fish, down to a near-identical taste and delicacy, but with a profoundly environmental twist – it's not fish!

According to their website, the company explain, "We start with widely available, affordable, unprocessed organic matter and add a nutrient-rich solution to 'feed' and nurture the microbes. We then introduce a strain of fungi to begin the transformation. By controlling environmental factors like heat, humidity and moisture –

and nailing the formula – the end result is a whole protein with a realistic texture and taste to traditional seafood."

These kinds of innovation could have huge consequences for the sushi industry, steering it away from environmentally harmful fishing demands and towards a sustainable future. Long live green sushi!

YOU MAKI
ME SO HAPPY

SUSHI TAKES ON PIRACY

Japanese sushi chain CEO Kiyoshi Kimura significantly contributed to a drop-off in piracy off the coast of Somalia by offering the would-be pirates an alternative means of income – training them up to become sushi-grade tuna fishermen. The men had largely been forced into piracy due to civil war in their homeland and were grateful for Kimura's intervention.

THE
BIG NAMES

From sushi heavyweights like the instantly recognizable maki rolls available in elite sushi restaurants and grocery stores alike, to colourful boats of gunkan, delicious bowls of chirashi and fiery dragon rolls, there are as many variations of sushi as there are tastes.

In this chapter, prepare to meet the giants of the sushi world and discover their fascinating origin stories, offering an idea of their flavour and composition. By the time you've finished, you'll be a pro, and distinguishing between maki and futomaki in your sleep.

Sushi Profile: Maki

Description: The word "maki", or the Japanese name makizushi, refers to sushi rice that has been rolled to give it its signature round shape. Maki rolls can take many forms, but they all share a common circular shape and are wrapped together using nori seaweed. Typically, maki are served with soy sauce for dipping. There are no rules when it comes to filling maki, meaning they can be enjoyed by anyone, and never get boring – the perfect cuisine for experimental eaters.

Common ingredients: Sushi rice, nori, vegetables, salmon

Did you know? While nori seaweed is the wrapper of choice for maki-style sushi, it's not the only option. Egg, thinly sliced cucumber or even soy paper can be used as alternatives, offering fresh textures and surprising flavour combinations.

Maki

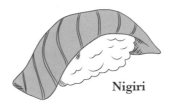

Nigiri

Uramaki

YOU ARE SOY AWESOME!

Sushi Profile: Nigiri

Description: Translating as "two fingers", nigiri is one of the most distinctive sushi varieties. Made up of a chilled, oval mound of rice with a delicate slice of fish or seafood placed on top, it's popular the world over. The fish used for nigiri, often tuna, yellowtail or salmon, is almost always raw, with a thin layer of wasabi pasted between the fish and the rice as a garnish, or to add flavour and heat. Due to the simplicity of the ingredients and construction, nigiri is considered one of the purest and oldest forms of sushi in the world.

Common ingredients: Sushi rice, salmon, shrimp, tuna, yellowtail, wasabi

Did you know? As its translation suggests, nigiri isn't traditionally eaten using chopsticks – using your hands is considered more polite. And perhaps more surprisingly, sushi etiquette favours that you eat these tasty pieces in one bite. Get stuck in!

Sushi Profile: Uramaki

Description: Take everything you know about sushi and turn it inside out - literally - for a delicious uramaki roll, sometimes known as the "rebel roll". These dishes are created with the nori seaweed wrapped tightly around the inner ingredients, then surrounded by a roll of rice, often garnished with sesame seeds. Uramaki is one of the most complex varieties of sushi for masters to create due to its unusual composition.

Common ingredients: Sushi rice, nori seaweed, salmon, avocado, sesame seeds

Did you know? Uramaki originated in the US during the 1960s, when much of the American population was intimidated by seaweed, then still considered an exotic and strange ingredient. Nori was concealed inside the roll to make sushi more palatable. Despite these creative solutions, 32% of Americans have still never tried sushi.

SUSHI ON THE MOVE

Conveyor-belt restaurants are one of the most fun ways to enjoy sushi. Known as *kaiten zushi* in Japan, they were invented by innovator Yoshiaki Shiraishi, who was inspired by beer bottles he saw on a conveyor belt at a brewery. His technology ensured sushi could be mass-produced, and therefore more became affordable and accessible to the masses.

Sushi Profile: Chirashi

Description: Chirashi sushi is presented not in rolls, cones or wraps, but completely deconstructed. A bed of sushi rice is placed in a bowl or box with a variety of ingredients "scattered" over the top – this could range from shiitake mushrooms to shrimp paste or raw fish. The doll festival, *Hinamatsuri*, is a popular occasion for enjoying chirashi sushi. Celebrated on 3 March, *Hinamatsuri* is a religious day dedicated to prayers for the happiness and prosperity of female relatives.

Common ingredients: Sushi rice, fish cakes, shiitake mushrooms, lotus root, cucumber

Did you know? There are two principal types of chirashi sushi: edomae and bara chirashi. Edomae, or Toyko-style, is the most popular, and includes lots of seafood, both raw and cooked. Bara on the other hand, uses smaller pieces of seafood, which have been marinated. Chirashi is often credited as the inspiration behind the modern-day sashimi bowl.

Chirashi

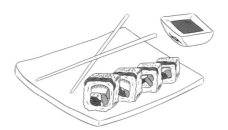

Dragon Roll

Sushi Profile: Dragon roll

Description: Dragon rolls are a festive form of uramaki sushi. Instead of placing the rolls side by side on a platter, they're served lined up, stood directly behind each other to give the presentation the snaking appearance of Japanese dragon dance costumes. Dragon rolls are often (but not always) decorated with thin slices of cucumber or avocado to give the additional appearance of dragon-like scales.

Common ingredients: Sushi rice, nori seaweed, cucumber, avocado, wasabi

Did you know? Dragon roll is one of the most popular sushi styles in the United States, perhaps thanks to its fun, festive appearance. There are many varieties of the dragon roll, with many leaning into the theatricality of its name. The black dragon roll uses serrano peppers and peppered tuna for a fiery kick, while the phoenix dragon roll incorporates crab, avocado and eel.

Sushi Profile: Temaki

Description: Temaki is hand-rolled sushi, very distinctive from maki-style sushi in its larger size (usually around 10-cm long) and cone shape, perfectly designed to eat with your hands. Rolled into a tubular shape and wrapped in a large sheet of nori seaweed, temaki sushi is eaten rather like an ice cream cone, rather than the classic dainty chopsticks method of eating maki. It is far more common to use cooked fish such as smoked salmon or fried shrimp in its construction than it is in other traditional forms of sushi.

Common ingredients: Sushi rice, nori seaweed, smoked salmon, shrimp tempura

Did you know? Temaki first appeared in the nineteenth century in the street food kiosks of Tokyo. The conical shape was created to avoid the sushi filling from spilling onto the fast-food lover's clothes.

Sushi Profile: Sashimi

Description: Though not technically sushi, sashimi is frequently offered in sushi restaurants and served up alongside its rice-heavy cousins. Often presented with daikon radish, pickled ginger, wasabi and soy sauce, sashimi consists of delicate, thinly cut raw food, most commonly fish. It's usually offered as the first course or a starter before a main meal. Sashimi only refers to the raw item itself – if a dish is served with rice, it's not sashimi. Sashimi takes considerable skill to prepare – very sharp knives and an attention to the fineness and delicacy of your cut are the order of the day.

Common ingredients: Salmon, tuna, squid, beef, octopus, horse, pork, flounder

Did you know? Sashimi should be eaten as daintily as it is presented – using chopsticks and dipped in a generous bath of soy sauce or citrusy ponzu.

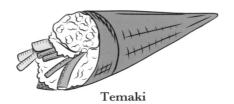

Temaki

Sashimi

SPOILED FOR CHOICE

Tokyo is home to the largest number of
restaurants in the world, with a whopping 150,000
different venues in the city. By comparison,
the mecca of world food, New York, has
just 27,000. Tokyo is also home to the most
Michelin-starred restaurants of any city in the
world (230 at last count), so if it's elite sushi
you're looking for, you know where to go.

Sushi Profile: Gunkan

Description: The word "gunkan" roughly translates as "war boat", the perfect name for these stout little sushi portions. Gunkan consists of tightly packed sushi rice formed by hand and wrapped in nori seaweed to create a fillable boat shape, usually packed full of fish eggs, crab, squid, avocado and other delights. Outside of Japan, gunkan is often the sushi that invites the most experimentation. Look hard enough and you'll find toppings as strange as quail eggs, beef tartar or mushrooms and mayonnaise.

Common ingredients: Sushi rice, nori seaweed, fish eggs, crab, squid, avocado

Did you know? Gunkan is a relatively modern addition to the pantheon of great sushi, originating in 1941 in the legendary Tokyo sushi restaurant, Kyubey. The restaurant still exists today, making it something of a pilgrimage spot for sushi lovers from across the world.

Sushi Profile: The California Roll

Description: This maki sushi is usually rolled inside out in the uramaki style and filled with crabsticks, cucumber, avocado and mayonnaise. The outside of the roll is sometimes also sprinkled with fish roe or gently toasted sesame seeds.

Common ingredients: Sushi rice, nori, sesame seeds, mayonnaise, crabsticks, cucumber, avocado

Did you know? This American fusion invention was most likely birthed in Los Angeles, though chefs from Canada have also laid claim to its creation. However they came to be, California Rolls are one of the world's most enduringly popular fusion sushi orders. Offering a combination of familiar and unfamiliar flavours, they are thought to have played a big part in launching sushi's popularity across the globe.

Gunkan

California Roll

Temarizushi

Sushi Profile: Temarizushi

Description: These cute-as-a-button sushi balls are traditionally prepared and enjoyed on 3 March to celebrate Japan's Hinamatsuri (Doll Festival) alongside colourful bowls of chirashi. To prepare temarizushi, sushi rice is rolled into a ball with your favourite ingredients and then topped with enticing ingredients such as tuna, seabream or colourful vegetables. This style of sushi is perfect for parties thanks to its playful composition and colourful appearance. Its unusual shape also lends a sense of variety to a platter of freshly prepared sushi.

Common ingredients: Sushi rice, salmon, tuna, seabream, vegetables

Did you know? Temarizushi's namesake, temari, are traditional Japanese embroidered balls, once used as children's toys but now more commonly found as household decorations.

Sushi Profile: Futomaki

Description: Your favourite sushi goes Godzilla with these supersized rolls. Very similar in appearance to a classic maki roll, the futomaki is a much fatter sushi, with twice as much rice and supersized fillings. The thickness of this sushi roll makes it a good starter dish for an amateur sushi itamae (meaning "chef" or "cook"), as the larger size allows for any slack in rolling, and over-ambitious quantities! Over a hundred years old, futomaki is one of the most traditional forms of sushi.

Common ingredients: Sushi rice, nori, salmon, tuna, spinach, omelette, cucumber, mushrooms, pickled plum

Did you know? The most popular traditional form of futomaki is eaten during *Setsubun*, a day of Japanese celebration that ushers in springtime, when it's considered a lucky dish. The full name of the dish, futomaki matsuri sushi, literally translates as "festive thick roll sushi".

Sushi Profile: Saiku maki

Description: One of the most playful forms of sushi, saiku maki, or kazari sushi, is a type of decorative roll often designed to look like flowers, popular cartoon characters or family crests. These sushi rolls are all about the looks, with priority given to aesthetic over taste (though you'd be hard pressed to stumble across one you wouldn't willingly tuck into!). A quick Google image search will show you a host of creative designs, from Halloween pumpkins to penguin faces to much-loved Studio Ghibli characters.

Common ingredients: Sushi rice, nori, tuna, squid ink, avocado

Did you know? There have been saiku maki competitions in Japan since the beginning of the Shōwa era (1926), and classes teaching their creation and art have become increasingly popular in recent years.

Futomaki

Saiku Maki

Rainbow Roll

Sushi Profile: Rainbow roll

Description: Perhaps the most Instagram-friendly sushi, the rainbow roll is an uramaki sushi roll that uses colourful ingredients on the outside to give it an extremely fresh and aesthetically pleasing, not to mention appetizing, look. Ingredients that create a strong colour contrast are the name of the game, such as punchy orange salmon next to lush green avocado. Fillings for rainbow rolls generally owe more to American sushi offerings than they do to traditional Japanese fare, with roasted peppers, mayonnaise, creamy avocado and crabsticks all serving as popular ingredients. The idea is to get your roll as colourful as possible! Definitely one to show off at your next dinner party.

Common ingredients: Sushi rice, nori, salmon, avocado, crabsticks, cucumber, yellowtail

Did you know? These rolls are a popular choice when catering for Pride parties, as their colourful and diverse appearance lends itself perfectly to a celebratory rainbow aesthetic.

Sushi Profile: Narezushi

Description: One of the oldest forms of sushi in the world, and yet one some modern tastes may find less palatable, narezushi is truly a dish for the die-hard sushi fan. Using fish preserved for several months in salt and rice, narezushi is a throwback to the very earliest days of sushi, when the cuisine was a way to preserve the life of seafood, rather than the flavourful art it has grown into today. In original forms of narezushi, the rice was discarded before eating the fish, but today fish and rice are enjoyed as one, in a very pungent-tasting dish. Perhaps not one to make at home.

Common ingredients: Sushi rice, fermented nigorobuna fish

Did you know? The most popular form of narezushi is made using nigorobuna fish caught from Lake Biwa in Honshu. This dish takes five years to ferment and commands a suitably high price, meaning it's considered something of a delicacy.

Sushi Profile: Oshizushi

Description: Looking something like a sushi ice cream sandwich, the rectangular blocks of oshizushi are a popular form of "pressed sushi" in which a variety of toppings are carefully layered on sushi rice and pressed together using a special mould. The mould uses weights to compress the layers of the sushi together, creating a tightly packed block of deliciousness.

Common ingredients: Sushi rice, raw fish, egg, mushroom, kelp

Did you know? Oshizushi can be found across all of Japan, with different regions offering different takes on the traditional dish. In Osaka, mackerel is the star ingredient, and layers are so thin that they're almost see through. In Nagasaki, layers of scrambled egg offer an unusual texture. In Tottori, the pressed sushi is wrapped in a layer of kelp.

Narezushi

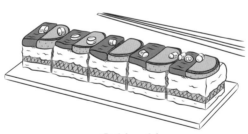

Oshizushi

SO MANY ROLLS,
SO LITTLE TIME...

The Sushi Dictionary

- **Agari:** Head to a traditional Japanese sushi bar and you may hear this word used to refer to green tea, a popular accompaniment.

- **Bara:** When sushi ingredients are combined in a bowl with rice as a salad.

- **Daikon:** A common sushi garnish, daikons are large white radishes frequently served with sashimi.

- **Gari:** Pickled ginger often served as a side to sushi and used as a palate cleanser between rolls.

- **Gohan:** The Japanese term for plain rice. Salt, rice vinegar and sugar must be added before it becomes sushi rice.

- **Hashi:** The Japanese word for "chopsticks". While not mandatory for every sushi dish, they're the traditional and polite way to eat many varieties, including maki rolls.

- **Hocho:** The sharp knives used for preparing fish for sushi.

- **Makisu:** The bamboo mat used for rolling sushi. An essential in any sushi master's armoury.

- **Mirin:** A sweet Japanese wine often used to add a depth of flavour to marinades used for many sushi ingredients.

- **Miso:** A paste made from fermented soybean that has a strong umami flavour. Frequently used in soups, sauces and marinades.

- **Neta:** The raw piece of fish that is placed on top of oval-shaped rice to create nigiri sushi.

- **Nori:** The thin sheets of seaweed used to wrap sushi rolls.

- **Oshibori:** If you've been to a lot of sushi restaurants, you'll be accustomed to oshibori – the wet towel you're offered to clean your hands with before a meal.

- **Panko:** Flaky breadcrumbs often used as a topping or coating for sushi rolls to add texture.

- **Ponzu:** A sweet dipping sauce for sushi.

- **Sake:** Traditional, distilled Japanese rice wine routinely served with sushi.

- **Shoyu:** Soy sauce, popular for dipping sushi rolls, made from fermented soy beans.
- **Tamago:** The Japanese term for egg. This usually refers to a sweetened omelette, sliced and used as sushi topping.
- **Tempura:** The act of battering and frying; in sushi, this is usually done to shrimp or vegetables.
- **Wasabi:** A green horseradish-flavour paste that gives sushi heat.
- **Yakumi:** The Japanese term to refer to condiments.

HOW TO
EAT SUSHI

One of the most common reasons people are put off ordering or enjoying sushi is that they fear they won't know how to eat it. Will you end up having to request the fork of shame to enjoy your meal? Dropping your shrimp tempura deep in the soy sauce? Offending somebody with a rogue waggle of your chopstick?

Whether you're nervous about using chopsticks, performing the correct etiquette at dinner or which condiments to use and when, this chapter will put those anxieties to rest. From learning the components of a traditional sushi meal, to the correct order in which to eat your sushi, and the difference between a sushi-ya restaurant and a kaiten-zushi, the following pages have you covered. Finish this chapter and people will think you've been eating sushi since the cradle.

What makes a traditional sushi meal?

A traditional sushi meal is usually served at dinner. Typical meals may also include miso soup and a side of vegetables to compliment the sushi main. The table will usually host condiments alongside your sushi (soy sauce is standard) as well as wasabi to add spice and ginger as a palate cleanser.

Drink options to accompany sushi are many and varied. If you're looking for something traditional and sophisticated, then sake (a Japanese spirit made from fermented rice) makes for a refined pairing. If you're looking for something more comforting, then a steaming mug of green tea is perfect. Turn to page 88 for a full list of the best sushi drinks pairings.

Get clever with condiments

Great sushi can be enhanced through the addition of traditional condiments, which bring out the flavour and offer great palate cleansers between courses.

Of course, the accompaniment most people are familiar with is soy sauce. Splash a little onto your plate before tucking into your sushi, and to blend in with the pros, dip the fish side of your sushi into the soy sauce. Only amateurs dip their sushi rice-first!

Wasabi is always available to add a little kick to your sushi but proceed with caution. Use too much and you'll blow your mouth up, or worse, offend the chef who has painstakingly ensured just the right amount of wasabi has already been included in your dish.

The traditional way to eat sushi

The most common mistake modern diners make when eating sushi is to use chopsticks for everything. To eat sushi traditionally, you have to get a bit dirty. Speaking to the *Daily Mail*, Chef Nobuyuki "Nobu" Matsuhisa, founder of the world-famous Nobu restaurants, explained, "I like it when people eat sushi with their fingers because sushi chefs make the sushi with their fingers, and with their heart."

Perhaps the second most common mistake is overusing the soy sauce. Soy sauce contains high levels of sodium, so you should only pour a shallow amount into your bowl and lightly dab your sushi – not drench the entire roll.

Mixing wasabi into your soy sauce is another tell-tale sign of a sushi novice. According to *Business Insider*'s interview with Chef Matsuhisa, "the traditional Japanese way to eat wasabi with sushi is by dipping the piece of fish into a small amount of soy sauce and using your chopsticks or fingers to place some wasabi on the centre of the fish."

In Japan, sushi is traditionally eaten as part of celebrations, so the next time you get good news or want to mark a big birthday, head to your local sushi restaurant and let your order do the talking!

PROCEED GINGERLY

Ginger isn't a topping! Traditionally speaking, the pretty, pink pickled ginger that sits alongside your wasabi isn't meant to top your sushi but is intended as a palate cleanser between bites. If you want to enjoy your sushi the traditional way, try a bite of ginger between each roll. Still prefer ginger as a topping? Get stuck in. It's your sushi!

LET'S (CHOP)
STICK TOGETHER!

Sushi etiquette tips

Foodies who are apprehensive about adding sushi to their cuisine conquests often note the etiquette of Japanese dining as a barrier to their enjoyment. But eating sushi the polite way is easier than you might think.

First, clean hands are everything. If your server offers you a towel, use it! That way you can make the most of tucking in with your hands and simplifying your sushi experience.

Where possible, try to eat your sushi in one bite. Cutting it into pieces is considered rude.

There's also an order to eating sushi. Traditionally, sushi made with white fish is eaten first, then red fish and then any sushi containing egg.

And finally, never mix your soy sauce with your wasabi. Combining these condiments will risk spoiling both the flavours, not to mention offending your chef!

WHAT'S IN A NAME?

In 2021, a Taiwanese sushi restaurant ran a promotion offering free all-you-can-eat sushi to anyone with the Chinese characters for "salmon" in their name. Not about to pass on free sushi, hundreds of people legally changed their name to "salmon". Unfortunately, many didn't realize there were legal limits on how many times you could change your name, leaving them stuck with their new fishy moniker!

Where to eat sushi

When it comes to sushi restaurants, there's no one-size-fits-all. Sushi can be enjoyed from friendly street vendors as readily as it can in exclusive club houses, but there are different rules and expectations from different venues.

Sushi-ya restaurants are formal establishments that specialize in sushi. In most of these eateries, you'll be sat at a table or counter with a view of your sushi chef creating his masterpieces. Most of these locations offer a-la-carte menus and allow diners to enjoy appetizers and drinks before their main course.

Kaiten zushi restaurants are less expensive and the sushi on offer is often presented on a conveyor belt, allowing customers to pick and choose their order. These venues aren't formal at all and are a popular place to enjoy a casual sushi lunch. Despite the less formal atmosphere, etiquette is still important – never return a partly eaten sushi plate to the belt and make sure you aren't helping yourself to more sushi than you're able to eat.

HAVE A
RICE DAY!

Chopstick etiquette and tips

How to use chopsticks: Hold your first chopstick between
the base of your thumb and your ring finger, to create
a stable position. Then, place your second chopstick
between your first and second finger and the tip of your
thumb, much like holding a pencil. To pick up food,
move the top chopstick up and down.

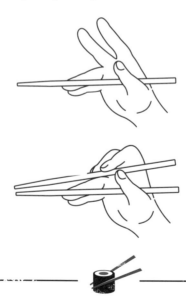

If you wish to use chopsticks to enjoy your meal, there are certain etiquette rules it's important to observe:

1. Don't rub chopsticks together. This implies you're trying to get rid of splinters in your chopsticks because they're cheap – very rude to the establishment you're dining in.

2. Never pass food between chopsticks. Instead, place the food down for your companion to pick up themselves (see page 80).

3. Always use two chopsticks. Using just one chopstick to spear your food is a sushi faux pas.

4. Chopsticks aren't for gesturing. Using your chopstick to gesture is as rude as using your finger to point at someone.

5. Resist chopstick wavering. Rather than hovering over the sushi before you, take a moment to choose your next dish and move towards it directly.

ELITE EATERY ETIQUETTE

If you're lucky enough to enjoy sushi in Japan, avoid this major mistake. Passing food from one set of chopsticks to another is considered highly taboo, as this is the way the bones of the deceased are passed during traditional Japanese funeral rituals. If you want your company to try your rolls, put them onto their plate first instead!

Sushi lunchboxes

Each year a staggering five billion lunchboxes are made at home in Japan, and the parents preparing them for their families regularly go viral for sharing their creative and eye-catching designs on the internet.

Known as bento boxes, Japanese lunchboxes are compartmentalized containers with different sections for snacks, vegetables and of course, sushi. Chara-ben – packed lunches made to look like characters from films, TV, cute creatures or even real people – are the most popular of these viral creations, and often use their distracting aesthetics to encourage children to eat the kinds of healthy food they'd usually turn their nose up at.

Users creating videos of their sushi box designs on social media app TikTok frequently go viral thanks to the satisfying nature of their craft. For inspiration for your own sushi lunchbox, check out the TikTok hashtag #SushiBentoBox and the tasty recipes in the next chapter of this book.

Keeping up appearances

Japanese cuisine is known the world over for its meticulous standards of presentation, and nowhere is this more evident than in its sushi restaurants. There are many different aesthetics when it comes to serving sushi, from the traditional use of minimalistic lacquer plates to detailed images created in the rice. Here are a few of the most famous.

- **Kazari maki:** This intricate presentation style uses the ingredients of the sushi to create elaborate floral patterns, bright colour combinations or to create the faces of well-known cartoon or movie characters.

- **Kaiten-zushi:** Conveyor-belt sushi changed the sushi industry forever, allowing restaurants to serve a greater volume of people than ever before. This is commonly found in less formal dining establishments, offering a budget-friendly way to enjoy sushi.

- **Nyotaimori:** *Sex and the City* fans know this one all too well. Nyotaimori refers to sushi served on the body of a naked woman. The heat of the woman's body raises the temperature of the sushi, supposedly creating a unique mouthfeel. Unsurprisingly, this is usually relegated to "seedy" establishments in Japan and has fallen even further from favour in recent years as more diners are outraged by the objectification of this process.

- **Omakase:** Feeling adventurous? Asking to eat omakase means giving your sushi chef free reign to prepare whatever creation they like, served in any manner they see fit. So sit back, relax and prepare to be surprised.

MASTER OF THE ART

Born in 1925, Japanese chef Jiro Ono (star of the documentary *Jiro Dreams of Sushi*) is considered the greatest living sushi master. His three Michelin star restaurant, Sukiyabashi Jiro, is one of the toughest in the world to get a reservation at and has hosted a wealth of famous guests, including Barack Obama, who said of the experience, "I was born in Hawaii and ate a lot of sushi, but this was the best sushi I've ever had in my life."

JUST ROLL
WITH IT!

Novelty sushi

With sushi now well known and loved across the globe, more unusual ways of enjoying the dish are cropping up than ever before.

Head to Portland, Oregon in the United States, and you could try the surprising flavours of insect sushi, served with intact creepy crawlies on top of thin slices of nigiri. Chef Shoichi Uchiyama of Diner Echo offers sushi garnished with a topping choice of locusts, scorpions, caterpillars or even cockroaches.

Located off an unassuming side street in Tokyo, restaurant Sushiya no Nohachi has gained notoriety for their eccentric sushi serves. There are seven varieties of "tiny sushi" on offer here, including sushi small enough to be served on a single grain of rice – all served free with an order of regular sized sushi.

Love sushi? Love waffles? The two have had a love-it-or-hate-it love child over at Mumbai's Technikue restaurant. The waffle shells are topped with both savoury and sweet ingredients, including eggs and fruit, and can even be topped with syrup.

LIFE HAPPENS.
SUSHI HELPS.

What to drink with sushi?

To complete your sushi feast, you'll want to pair your creations with some tasty drinks. Here are some of the most popular accompaniments.

- **Koshu:** A crisp, clean white wine is one of the best accompaniments to a plate full of fresh sushi. Koshu is made in Japan and is well stocked across the world.

- **Ginger ale:** Ginger isn't only great as a palate cleanser – it can be enjoyed as a delicious drink pairing to sushi too. An ice-cold refreshing glass of ginger ale will cool even the hottest wasabi kick.

- **Japanese beer:** Light lagers make for an unintrusive pairing with sushi, and there are plenty of international imports of Japanese brands such as Asahi and Hitachino Nest.

- **Green tea:** Don't fancy something alcoholic? Not only is green tea a tasty accompaniment to your meal, but it doubles up as a palate cleanser between sushi rolls. Sencha is a popular variety of green tea in Japan and has an appetizing nutty aroma.

- **Sake:** Pick a bottle polished to 50% or less to ensure the taste of your sushi is still the dominant flavour. Rice used to brew sake is polished in order to remove unnecessary components. The higher the percentage, the purer the sake.

DESTINED TO MISS OUT

Back in 1998, a neuroscience professor at
Stanford University found that if you've never
eaten sushi by the age of 39 there's a 95%
chance that you never will. This is because
as we age, we are less receptive to "novelty"
and therefore less likely to try new things.

Sushi bar etiquette

Going to your first sushi bar is exciting, but just as there are etiquette rules when it comes to eating sushi, there are rules around your conduct in these kinds of venues too, particularly if you're lucky enough to be enjoying sushi in Japan.

Always ask before taking photographs. As beautiful and exciting as the sushi bar may be, it's considered very rude to take photos – particularly those involving your sushi chef – without first asking permission.

Avoid wearing strong perfume. As fragrance is key to the enjoyment of sushi and traditional bars are often cosy establishments, it's polite to avoid wearing overpowering scents as they can detract from people's enjoyment of their food.

Order little by little. It's considered insulting to the chef to not finish the food that you order, so to avoid eyes bigger than your stomach, order in smaller courses, adding sushi as your appetite grows. That way there are no half-empty plates and no hurt feelings!

MAKING
SUSHI

"Making sushi is an art, and experience is everything." So says sushi master and founder of the legendary Nobu restaurant chains, Nobu Matsuhisa. And so says this chapter, where you will be introduced to some quintessential recipes to provide the foundation for mastering the art of sushi.

There's the American favourite California roll, the deeply traditional chirashi bowl and fun surprises such as gunkan "battleship" sushi, colourful temari balls and vegan takes on the classics. So, start up your rice cooker, prepare your sharpest knife and unfurl that bamboo mat – it's time for a sushi-tastic dinner party.

Key equipment

- **Bamboo mat:** Also known as the makisu, bamboo mats are crucial for creating tightly rolled sushi, but also for squeezing every drop of moisture out of wet ingredients, such as omelettes.

- **Cutting board:** Opt for something scratch and stain resistant with a synthetic surface that makes it easier to clean and less harsh on your knife edge.

- **Rice cooker:** A rice cooker ensures your sushi rice will always be cooked to perfection and will keep your rice warm for longer if it's taking you a while to perfect your meat cuts. There's a huge range of models on the market, so there should be something to suit every budget.

- **Serving set:** There's no point making beautiful food without something beautiful to serve it on. Treat yourself to a traditional serving set, which generally includes a square plate, smaller plate for condiments, chopsticks and a chopstick rest.

- **Shamoji:** This is a large flat spoon used to mix your rice after cooking, allowing moisture to escape. Traditional shamoji are made from bamboo.

- **Sharp knife:** Perhaps the most important tool in your armoury, you'll use this to cut very thin slices of raw fish. The sharper the better. Look out for knives with a line of dimples down the side as these prevent the fish from sticking to the blade.

- **A sharpening stone:** Key to keeping your knife sharp is a high-quality sharpening stone to ensure they don't lose their edge.

Key ingredients

- **Cucumber:** Few sushi recipes won't be improved with the addition of cucumber. This versatile vegetable is great wrapped tightly in a roll or served as a side.

- **Ginger:** This classic ingredient is a staple of every sushi table. The best sushi ginger is sweet, mild and pickled.

- **Nori sheets:** Roasted seaweed is an important part of most sushi recipes. Don't be afraid to bulk buy these seaweed sheets as they can keep fresh for up to a year in an airtight container.

- **Rice vinegar:** This is an essential ingredient for seasoning your sushi rice. Choose Japanese rice vinegar to keep your sushi as authentic as possible.

- **Soy sauce:** The ideal condiment for dipping your sushi. Serve in a small bowl.

- **Sushi-grade fish:** Only the freshest cuts of fish are suitable for creating truly delicious sushi. Try red tuna, salmon and shrimp for starters, and visit your local fishmonger for the best cuts.

- **Sushi rice:** Sushi rice is different from regular rice – its grain is shorter; it requires less water to cook and has a sticky quality perfect for forming sushi rolls.

- **Wasabi paste:** Bright green wasabi paste is a spicy must-have for sushi lovers.

Key techniques

- **Cooking sushi rice:** At least 50% of your sushi is rice, so it needs to be perfect. Using a rice cooker is the easiest way to ensure your rice is spot on, but there are other tricks to imitate the Japanese masters, such as only using a wooden bowl and spoon to prepare it. These are less harsh than metal tools so they keep your rice grains soft and intact.

- **Rolling sushi:** There's an art to perfectly rolled sushi, and the bamboo mat is your best friend when it comes to trying to achieve it. Dampen your hands to prevent rice from sticking, take a deep breath and go in with confidence – the mat can sense your fear.

- **Slicing for nigiri:** The handsome slices of fish you see proudly sitting atop restaurant-standard nigiri are much harder to achieve than they might look. Practice makes perfect, but working with the sharpest, highest quality knife you can afford is a good place to start.

- ☞ **Using a shamoji (bamboo spoon):** When you've finished cooking your rice in a rice cooker, add the rice vinegar mixture and combine with the shamoji, using a gentle stirring motion so as not to damage the delicate grains.

Measurements

The recipes in this chapter use metric measurements, but if you prefer using imperial (and you don't have a smartphone to do the conversions for you), here are some basic tables:

25 g ≈ 1 oz	15 ml ≈ ½ fl oz
60 g ≈ 2 oz	30 ml ≈ 1 fl oz
85 g ≈ 3 oz	75 ml ≈ 2½ fl oz
115 g ≈ 4 oz	120 ml ≈ 4 fl oz
255 g ≈ 9 oz	270 ml ≈ 9 fl oz

Making sushi

SUSHI
RECIPES

Basic sushi rice

Master the rice and you're already halfway towards your goal of perfect sushi. Good sushi rice should be fluffy and short-grained with a slightly sweet and sour flavour.

Makes enough for 10 sushi rolls

INGREDIENTS

250 g sushi rice

30 ml rice vinegar

20 g sugar

10 g salt

METHOD

Place your sushi rice in a bowl and cover it with water. Stir until the water turns cloudy, drain, and return to the bowl. Repeat until the water runs clear.

Drain your rice and add it to your rice cooker with 300 ml of water. Cook as per appliance instructions.

As your rice cooks, put your rice vinegar, sugar and salt in a small pan and heat until the ingredients have combined.

Remove the rice from your cooker, mix in the rice vinegar mixture with a shamoji, and set aside to cool.

Tuna nigiri

Colourful red tuna makes this nigiri one of the more iconic sushi recipes.

Serves 4

INGREDIENTS

280 g cooked sushi rice
200 g the finest quality tuna you can afford
Wasabi

METHOD

Carefully slice your tuna into 12 even pieces using a sharp dampened knife. Aim for slices to be an inch wide and the length and thickness of your longest finger.

Squeeze about three tablespoons of rice until it forms the classic long nigiri shape, slightly smaller than the slices of tuna you have prepared.

Spread a small dot of wasabi on the underneath of your tuna slice and press it onto the rice, with the rice on the top of the fish. This will ensure your roll is bonded.

Turn nigiri over and serve.

Vegan uramaki

This contemporary vegan take on a sushi classic uses the deep flavour of mushrooms to provide a tasty one-bite treat.

Serves 4

INGREDIENTS

350 g cooked sushi rice
2 sheets nori seaweed
70 g cooked chestnut mushrooms, sliced
70 g cooked shiitake mushrooms, sliced
70 g courgette, cut into thin strips
70 g carrots, cut into thin strips
Sesame seeds

METHOD

Cover your bamboo sushi mat with cling film and place the nori seaweed on it ensuring the shiny side is facing downwards.

Spread the rice over the middle section of the nori. Cover the rice in a light sprinkling of sesame seeds and press down so it's well bonded to the nori.

Flip your nori and rice so that it's now lying rice-down on the mat. Evenly spread your vegetables over the nori and then start to roll your bamboo mat, ensuring it is well compressed.

Unroll, slice into 10–12 even pieces and serve.

Gunkan

This "battleship" style gunkan sushi recipe is extremely visually appealing, and delicious to boot. Plus, it's surprisingly easy to make at home. Here's how.

Serves 2

INGREDIENTS

180 g cooked sushi rice
4 sheets nori seaweed
1 tablespoon salmon roe
1 tablespoon trout roe
30 g avocado, cut into small cubes
Wasabi

METHOD

Using damp hands, shape a small handful (about 25 g) of sushi rice into a compact oval shape.

Cut your nori sheets lengthways into strips of approximately one inch wide. Wrap each nori strip around the outside of your sushi rice oval so that roughly half the strip overlaps with the rice at the top, creating a sort of cup. Dampen the end of the strip and adhere it to itself.

Dab a small amount of wasabi to the top of your rice. Carefully fill each gunkan with your preferred ingredients. For a classic style, stick to one ingredient per gunkan, or if you're feeling creative, try a combination.

Temarizushi

These colourful ball-shaped sushi are commonly made for celebrations in Japan. Why not serve them up at your next dinner party or birthday?

Serves 3 (roughly 9 balls)

INGREDIENTS

250 g cooked sushi rice
100 g finely cut salmon
100 g cucumber
100 g shrimp/prawns
100 g avocado
Wasabi

METHOD

Arrange a thin layer of toppings on a piece of cling film wrap, topside down.

With moist fingers or a spoon, place about 25 g of sushi rice directly on top of the toppings.

Bring the cling film corners together above your ingredients and twist them together so that they begin to compact the ingredients. Keep doing this until they are tightly brought together in a ball shape, unwrap and voila! You have your first temarizushi ball. Repeat until you've used all your ingredients.

Vegan chirashi

Don't let sushi-purists gatekeep chirashi – you don't need to include meat or seafood for it to be both authentic and delicious. This recipe proves it!

Serves 2

INGREDIENTS

180 g cooked sushi rice

200 g finely sliced cucumber

125 g carrot, cut into thin matchsticks

50 g pink pickled onions

1 tablespoon fresh ginger

Small radish, very finely sliced

Wasabi

METHOD

Fill a large dining bowl with your sushi rice. Top in a neat pattern with your vegetables, either grouping together by kind or scattering for a more artsy presentation.

Add a spoonful of ginger to the corner of your bowl and garnish with the radish and a dab of wasabi.

Spicy tuna dragon roll

Serve this in its long roll form for a truly dramatic dish.

Makes 1 sushi roll

INGREDIENTS

150 g cooked sushi rice

3 tablespoons mayonnaise

1 tablespoon sriracha

60 g the highest quality red tuna you can afford, diced

1 sheet nori seaweed

1 packet crispy shallots

75 g cucumber, cut into thin strips

METHOD

Mix the mayonnaise and sriracha, then add tuna.

Cover your bamboo mat with cling film, place a nori sheet shiny side down, and cover with the rice. Add crispy shallots and gently press down.

Flip the nori sheet so the shallot side is now touching the cling film. Add a tuna, and then the cucumber.

Roll using your bamboo mat, then slice and serve!

Temaki

No bamboo mat is needed for this fun sushi recipe, a perfect choice if you want to get younger family members involved in making the dinner.

Serves 4

INGREDIENTS

250 g cooked sushi rice
4 sheets nori seaweed
80 g cucumber, sliced into thin strips
8 thin slices of fresh smoked salmon

METHOD

Cut your nori sheets in half to create two rectangle-shaped pieces.

Scoop a quarter of the rice onto the left half of the nori and gently flatten into a thin layer.

Top the rice with cucumber and two slices of salmon.

With water-moistened fingers, take the bottom left corner of the nori and fold it diagonally up across the fillings until you've formed a cone shape. At this point, the right-hand side of the nori will still be unwrapped. Next, take the remaining right-hand side of the nori and fold it so that it wraps around the cone shape. Eat immediately after making.

Struggling to master the cone shape? There's nothing to say temaki can't be enjoyed in a classic roll shape too.

California rolls

Try your hand at this world-favourite fusion sushi!

Serves 3

INGREDIENTS

300 g cooked sushi rice

100 g crabsticks, chopped

5 tablespoons mayonnaise

3 sheets nori seaweed

250 g cucumber, sliced into sticks

1 avocado, sliced

Sesame seeds to top

METHOD

Combine crabsticks and mayonnaise in a small bowl.

Lay your first sheet of nori on your bamboo mat and cover in a third of the rice. Dust with sesame seeds and gently press down.

Flip over, covering the reverse of the nori sheet in a third of the crabstick mixture and lay slices of cucumber and avocado on top. Roll using the bamboo mat. Unfurl and cut into even pieces. Repeat to make two more rolls.

Making sushi

SIDES AND
GARNISHES

Pickled ginger

Ginger is a popular ingredient in Japanese cuisine because of its medicinal properties. Pickled ginger, a sushi staple, is made from thin slices of young ginger brined in rice vinegar, salt and sugar. When consumed alongside wasabi, as it so often is during a sushi dinner, it is thought to aid digestion. It owes its pink colour to a reaction when the ginger comes into contact with the vinegar and sugar, although some restaurants add food dye to their pickle in order to present a more visually appealing sushi side.

To pickle your own ginger, peel and thinly slice fresh ginger and combine with two tablespoons of salt. Then add to a jar with 120 ml rice vinegar, two tablespoons of sugar and 250 ml of water. Wait at least two days before enjoying.

Ideal pairing: Pickled ginger works well as an addition to chirashi bowls, where it adds a tart flavour and fun, colourful visual.

Miso soup

This staple of Japanese cuisine can be enjoyed for breakfast, lunch and dinner. Touted as having great health benefits, a traditional miso soup is made from miso (a paste of fermented soya beans), tofu, dashi (a stock that forms the soup's base), onion, wakame seaweed, kombu seaweed and spring onions. There are many regional variations across Japan, meaning there are plenty of variations on the classic recipe that you can experiment with until you find the perfect broth for you.

Having a daily portion of miso soup is believed to encourage a healthy digestive system, provide the body with key nutrients such as magnesium, zinc and bone-strengthening minerals, and take care of your heart thanks to the rich cholesterol-reducing ingredients such as vitamin K.

Ideal pairing: Pair your miso soup with California rolls for a truly fusion meal. The refreshing, light flavours of the California roll pair well with the rich depth of the miso soup, and dipping the rolls into the broth makes for a surprisingly delicious combo!

Edamame

Edamame beans offer a wholly different textural experience to a sushi-heavy meal, making them the perfect pairing for a varied mouthfeel. These East Asian soybeans are rich in vitamins and can be prepared in a variety of ways, making them a versatile addition to your table. The health benefits of edamame include reducing breast cancer risk, lowering rates of heart disease and easing cholesterol.

The beauty of edamame is all in the seasoning. From the classic Himalayan salt sprinkling to a fiery spicy chilli, you can adapt the flavour depending on the dish you wish to pair it with. To eat your edamame, don't make the rookie mistake of placing the whole thing in your mouth. Instead, squeeze the beans out of their pods into a bowl, flavour or season to your preference, and enjoy!

Ideal pairing: Edamame beans are a classic pairing that cry out for a classic sushi. Serve them with simple maki rolls for a truly traditional meal.

Tempura

Increasingly, fusion dishes are serving tempura ingredients inside sushi rolls, but tempura still makes for a delicious – and impressive – pairing for several sushi dishes. Tempura is any food, most commonly seafood, meat or vegetables, that has been deep-fried in a batter of flour, egg and water. The crispy texture of tempura is unlike textures found in most sushi giving it an exciting mouthfeel when accompanied with the smoother textures found in classic sushi dishes such as nigiri.

Perhaps the biggest delight in tempura is that it's so surprisingly easy to make and can often be done with little to no advance planning, as its key ingredients tend to be store-cupboard staples. Get creative with your fillings! Shrimp, mushroom, courgette, seasoned chicken – they all make for delicious tempura options.

Ideal pairing: Make the most of tempura's unique texture and serve it with fresh nigiri rolls. That combination of smooth and crunchy is irresistible!

Cucumber salad

Cucumber has cropped up again and again as a key sushi ingredient in this book, and for good reason. Its fresh, light flavour and distinctive crunch makes it the perfect foil to the soft texture of sushi rice and intense flavours of the fish and sushi rice vinegar. Sunomono – Japanese cucumber salad – is a popular sushi accompaniment and very easy to construct.

Combine 60 ml rice vinegar with half a teaspoon each of salt and sugar in a bowl and add two very thinly sliced cucumbers and a sprinkling of sesame seeds and you're finished. Simple to make yet delicious and aesthetically pleasing.

Not only is this salad healthy and fresh, but it's extremely moreish, making it a sushi side you'll return to time and time again.

Ideal pairing: To let this salad really shine, avoid pairing it with other sushi where cucumber is a dominant ingredient, such as fish roe gunkan. It adds a great dose of authenticity to fusion sushi like California or dragon rolls.

Seaweed salad

Think of sushi and you think of seaweed, so of course a classic seaweed salad had to be included in this pick of sushi sides. Known as "wakame", a Japanese-style seaweed salad is green, vibrant and packed full of flavour. Wakame has been consumed for thousands of years in Japan, with a history so rich that traces of this ingredient have been found in Japanese pottery artefacts dating back as far as at least 300 BC.

Using dried seaweed works really well for this dish as it rehydrates easily in water and can be stored for longer between usage. For this simple salad, salted wakame seaweed and sesame seeds are tossed in a dressing of:

Soy sauce (to taste)
1 tablespoon rice vinegar
1 teaspoon sugar
1 tablespoon olive oil

1 teaspoon grated ginger
½ teaspoon grated garlic

Ideal pairing: Seaweed salad makes a zingy addition to a serving of vegan uramaki (page 104), offering vibrant diversity of colour to your plate.

Conclusion

So, you've completed your magical mystery tour of the world of sushi. From humble origins to a cuisine that's dominated the world, we've traced sushi through its history from the rice paddies of Ancient China to elite restaurants in every corner of the modern world.

You've learned the perfect etiquette for enjoying a sushi meal and you've mastered some of the quintessential sushi dishes. Before you know it, you'll garner a reputation for throwing sushi dinner parties with beautifully colourful fresh dishes, and an in-depth knowledge of the food you're serving with some fun trivia bites to boot.

Having enjoyed this bite-size journey through sushi, the exciting news is that the adventure has only just begun. The best part of sushi is getting experimental. So now you've mastered the basics, get creative! See what innovations or fusions you can create yourself and use the hashtag #LittleBookOfSushi to share your genius with the world.

Nobody creates perfect sushi on the first try, and certainly not without making a mess of their kitchen in the process. The key to restaurant-worthy sushi is practice, practice, practice, and not being afraid to make a few messy mistakes along the way.

Top quality sushi is all about balance. All the components must speak to each other – thin fish, perfectly cooked rice, just enough rice vinegar. So, take a breath, channel your inner zen and take your time. The art is all part of the enjoyment.

And if everything goes wrong? Simply chalk it up to *wabi-sabi*, the Japanese aesthetic of accepting imperfection.

Resources

HISTORY OF SUSHI

jw-webmagazine.com/history-of-sushi/

www.sushisushi.co.uk/blogs/news/the-ancient-history-of-sushi

Podcast: The Untold Story of Sushi in America by The Daily

COOKING SUSHI

Free online courses from a sushi masterchef: www.openculture.com/2015/12/how-to-make-sushi-free-video-lessons-from-a-master-sushi-chef.html

www.dmagazine.com/food-drink/2013/03/5-tips-on-perfect-sushi-making-from-the-experts-at-nobu/

"Three Tips On Making Great Sushi From Chef Seizi Imura" by WBUR on YouTube

www.reveriepage.com/blog/expert-advice-that-will-help-you-make-a-perfect-sushi-at-home

www.forbes.com/sites/alywalansky/2022/06/15/celebrity-chefs-share-expert-tips-for-making-delicious-homemade-sushi/?sh=7e8596af665c

WHERE TO EAT SUSHI

www.sushifaq.com/sushiotaku/2006/05/27/how-to-find-a-good-sushi-restaurant/

www.thetravel.com/sushi-restaurants-best-world/

www.sushi-guide.co.uk/best-sushi-restaurants/

www.luxeat.com/blog/beginners-guide-fine-sushi-dining/

AND WHERE *NOT* TO EAT SUSHI...

www.thrillist.com/eat/nation/bad-sushi-crappy-sushi-joints

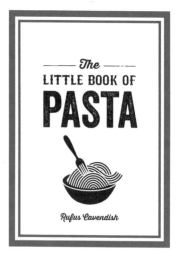

THE LITTLE BOOK OF PASTA

Rufus Cavendish

Paperback

978-1-80007-841-3

Whether fresh, dried, baked into lasagna or swirled as spaghetti around your fork, pasta is fantastic. From farfalle and fusilli to fettucine and beyond, this pocket guide serves up a celebration of one of the world's most popular foods. With history, trivia, tips and recipes, it's got all the information and inspiration you could hunger for.

THE LITTLE BOOK OF CURRY

Rufus Cavendish

Paperback

978-1-80007-417-0

From rogan josh and rendang to bunny chow and vindaloo, dive into this celebration of one of the world's most popular dishes: curry. Including the history of curry around the world, tips on growing your own spices, delicious recipes you can cook yourself and much more, *The Little Book of Curry* will help you spice up your life one dish at a time.

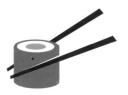

Have you enjoyed this book?
If so, find us on Facebook at
SUMMERSDALE PUBLISHERS, on Twitter at
@SUMMERSDALE and on Instagram and TikTok at
@SUMMERSDALEBOOKS and get in touch.
We'd love to hear from you!

WWW.SUMMERSDALE.COM